CONVERSATIONS WITH GOD

A Voice That Will Drive You Sane

CONVERSATIONS WITH GOD

A Voice That Will Drive You Sane

James R. Ryan

CBP Press

St. Louis, Missouri

Library of Congress Cataloging in Publication Data

Ryan, James Richard, 1943–
  Conversations with God.

  1. Christian life—1960—Addresses, essays,
lectures.   I. Title.
BV4501.2.R88   1984   248.4   84-7620

ISBN: 0-8272-0444-2

Printed in the United States of America

Contents

Acknowledgments

My sincere appreciation and admiration go to the members of First Chirstian Church whose openness to unique and varied forms of worship should serve as an example to congregations everywhere. Without their acceptance of these sermons, this series could obviously not have been developed.

A great deal of credit for the success of these sermons must go to Dr. Allan Lehl whose sensitive interpretation of the voice of God has made these sermons "work."

My deep appreciation is expressed to Ruth Swenson, administrative secretary, First Christian Church, for her expert typing of each sermon and the manuscript for this book. All ministers should be so lucky as to have a secretary of her quality.

And finally, my love and gratitude to my wife Pat and children Kent and Connie who have always supported me and who gave me encouragement in the beginning to experiment with this unique form of sermon.

Preface

"I am with you, always" is the promise that God makes to each of us, but do we really believe that, let alone internalize the reality of that promise? God with us at the office? God with us at the breakfast table? God with us as we relax in our easy chair? God with us at a party? Let us be honest. We spend a great deal of our day not even thinking about God, let alone being aware of God's presence.

If we were aware of God's presence and could actually hear God's voice, what would God be saying to us? What would God have to say about stress? What would God have to say about aging? What would God have to say about our responsibility in the world in which we live?

As human beings, we face many different situations, experiences and emotions in life. In this book, the voice of God breaks into our consciousness, providing new and often pointed insights and perspectives to the Christian faith and life.

The "conversations" were originally written as sermons for the members of First Christian Church, Des Moines, Iowa. The conversational approach provides a unique insight into the mind and will of God as it relates to the scriptures, Jesus and our role on earth as Christians. The first sermon was written in October of 1976. I have continued them at the rate of two per year. Members of the congregation often ask when the next "conversation" is scheduled.

Placing words in the mouth of God is a most delicate proposition and responsibility. Although I can never completely rid myself of my own biases, I have attempted to write these conversations out of my own understanding of the Scriptures and deep sense of faith in a God who is always present—even when we might prefer God to be absent.

—James R. Ryan

1
"You've Got to Be Kidding"

Psalm 139:7–10

(Jim walks out to the chancel. Chancel is set with a table, coffee cup, newspaper and chair.)

JIM: *(Looks out imaginary window.)* Rain! *(Looks at table, then off stage.)* Pat! Aren't you going to fix breakfast? *(Pause.)* She never has time for anything. *(Acts out pouring a cup of coffee. Sits down at table. Opens newspaper.)* Oh, great. More deaths. More killings. The stock market drops. God, what a morning!!

GOD: *(amplified voice offstage)* **It's a beautiful morning.**

JIM: *(looks around in disbelief)* It's a lousy morning.

GOD: **It's a morning I have made for you.**

JIM: You've got to be kidding. What is this? The FBI or CIA must have my kitchen bugged. Or one of my friends is playing a trick.

GOD: **Do you really think that's who I am?**

JIM: I've been working too hard. Now I'm hearing voices. Pat, I'm going to take a couple of days off next week.

GOD: She can't hear you. She's busy with the kids. It's just you and me.

JIM: It's not you and me. It's just me! I've been working too hard, and this is my self trying to tell myself to slow down. You are a voice from within.

GOD: I am who I am.

JIM: Wait a minute. That's what God said to Moses.

GOD: I know.

JIM: Are you trying to tell me that here I am in my own kitchen minding my own business and God is talking to me?

GOD: Does that surprise you?

JIM: Well, I think I could say that it is a little unexpected. Maybe if I were in the sanctuary at church . . . .

GOD: Why the sanctuary? Do you think that is the only place I am?

JIM: No, but . . . .

GOD: Did I not say I would be with you always?

JIM: Yes, but . . . .

GOD: Don't you believe that?

JIM: Well, I guess I hadn't really thought about it too much. But in my kitchen?

GOD: In your kitchen, in your office, on the tennis court, at parties . . . .

JIM: You mean you were with me last night?

GOD: Yes.

JIM: We had a good time, didn't we?

GOD: You seemed to be enjoying yourself.

JIM: Yes, I was. Didn't you have a good time?

GOD: I was a little concerned about Judy.

JIM: I noticed she seemed to be a little preoccupied last night. Kind of out of it. Like something was bothering her.

GOD: What was it?

JIM: I don't know. I didn't ask her.

GOD: Why not?

JIM: I was busy.

GOD: Haven't I asked you to care for people when they are in need?

JIM: Wait a minute. You're not going to make me feel guilty because I was enjoying myself and didn't ask Judy what her problem was.

GOD: Are you feeling guilty?

JIM: Why should I feel guilty? I was having a good time. Why should I pay attention to someone who is being a stick in the mud? Why should I have to be the one to talk to her and ask her what's wrong?

GOD: Why should you?

JIM: I don't know why me. There were other people there at the party. They could have talked to her. Look at Paul. He had a big time and he didn't bother talking to her. Why don't you bug him?

GOD: I'm talking to you now.

JIM: Why bug me? I do better than a lot of other people. What about Dave? He has really been nasty lately. He is so irritable. He's not even pleasant to be around. I do better than he does.

GOD: Did you know about his troubles at home?

JIM: No.

GOD: There usually is a reason for people's actions. He could use some understanding right now.

JIM: Well, anyway I try to be helpful and considerate. I try to smile and be pleasant and I think I do a better job of showing my concern than most people.

GOD: Do you think I grade on a scale like in school?

JIM: No, but . . . .

GOD: You seem to think that Christianity is a comparative religion, where if you are doing better than someone else, then that's all that's necessary. In Christianity, you don't match yourself up against someone else, you match yourself up against yourself.

JIM: Maybe you expect too much of me.

GOD: I know your capabilities. You are one of my creations. I want *you* to live as my Son has taught you.

JIM: But I'm not sure I can do that.

GOD: I am. *(Silence)*

JIM: Look, I believe in you. I do have a strong faith.

GOD: What is your faith?

JIM: I'm a Protestant. A member of the Christian Church (Disciples of Christ).

GOD: I didn't ask you what division of my church you belong to. I said, what is *your* faith?

JIM: I believe in you as God, my Father, as my Creator and Creator of this world. I believe that Jesus is the Christ, and he is Lord of my life.

GOD: That sounds nice. What does it mean to you?

12

JIM: Well, I guess . . . .

GOD: **I don't want guesses. I want to know what your faith means to you.**

JIM: Most importantly it means you love me. And I can love other people.

GOD: **Do you take that seriously?**

JIM: What do you mean do I take it seriously? Of course I do. I'm a Christian, aren't I?

GOD: **Are you?**

JIM: Yes. I said I believe in you and Jesus. I said I have faith.

GOD: **Is that all it takes to be a Christian?**

JIM: What else is there?

GOD: **You might try taking your faith seriously.**

JIM: I do take my faith seriously. I attend church meetings, I give money to the church . . . .

GOD: **Did you ask Judy if you could help last night?**

JIM: That's different. As I was saying, I help with the youth group . . . .

GOD: **Have you asked Dave what has been bothering him?**

JIM: No, but that's different, too.

GOD: **Is it?**

JIM: Well, what do you mean by taking my faith seriously?

GOD: **Through my Son I have asked you to live in a certain way. You said your faith means to you that my loving you enables you to love others. I want you to put that into action. I want to see you offering love, compassion, forgiveness, mercy, and joy to other people. I want you to put your faith into action.**

JIM: Oh.

GOD: **Do you think you are taking your faith seriously?**

JIM: Sometimes. Sometimes I really feel my faith and my capabilities as a Christian. I make a real effort at caring for others. But sometimes it seems as though my faith takes a hike and doesn't even enter my thinking, let alone my actions. Maybe there is room for improvement.

GOD: **Now we are starting to get somewhere.**

JIM: But you ask so much! You want me to be concerned about people when they are in need even when I'm having fun. You want me to quit viewing Christianity as a comparative religion and to use Jesus' teachings as my standards rather than how well someone else is doing. Basically, as I understand it, you want me to take my faith seriously and live that faith all the time.

GOD: **That's right.**

JIM: You've got to be kidding.

GOD: **When Jesus taught about love, peace, forgiveness, compassion and mercy he was not kidding. When he said, "You who are without sin cast the first stone," he was not kidding. When he said it is "better to give than to receive" he was not kidding. When he said, "Love your neighbor," he was not kidding. When he said, "What you do for the least of my brothers you do for me," he was not kidding. He went to the cross to prove he was not kidding. And I am not kidding.**

JIM: I believe you. I guess I'd better start taking my faith seriously, but right now I have to get ready for work. I'll talk to you again sometime. Good-by.

GOD: **You talk as if you're leaving me here in the kitchen.**

JIM: Well, I know you're busy and I have to get ready for work.

GOD: **I have said I will be with you always.**

JIM: I guess you weren't kidding. Perhaps that's the first thing that I should start taking seriously.

14

2
"Rocks in Your Cup"

Exodus 3:1–6,10—14a; 4:1,10

(Jim gives Children's Sermon with cup, rocks, candy bars. We often fill our lives with things of little lasting value and when God offers us something better we need to empty our cups of the old in order to fill our cups with the new. But that need not be a hardship; rather it can be a joy. Children leave. Jim stays there looking proud.)

GOD: That was very good.

JIM: *(Looks around very surprised. Meekly)* Thank you. Is that you?

GOD: I am who I am.

JIM: Yep, that's you! It's been three months since you talked to me. Where have you been?

GOD: I have been with you.

JIM: You have?

GOD: I am with you always.

JIM: That's what you said last time and I have been trying to take my faith seriously like you suggested but sometimes I forget.

GOD: I know.

JIM: Well, I have tried.

GOD: **Yes, at times you have and I appreciate those times. However, were you trying to take your Christian faith seriously last Thursday when you hurt Al's feelings? Were you trying to take your Christian faith seriously Friday when you yelled those words at that other driver? Were you trying to take your Christian faith seriously Friday night when . . . .**

JIM: Now wait a minute. There are people here and you're embarrassing me. Can't we talk about this some other time? This is a private matter.

GOD: **Your Christianity is a private matter?**

JIM: Well, no, I know my faith is supposed to be shared and that I'm supposed to live a Christian life, but I don't particularly want to be evaluated in front of all these people.

GOD: **The way you live is evaluated by people every day. They know whether you are living a Christian life.**

JIM: OK, OK. I know what you mean. The last time we talked was in my kitchen. What are you doing here in the sanctuary?

GOD: **You don't expect me to be here in the sanctuary during worship?**

JIM: Well . . . of course. We are here to worship you, to experience your presence . . . .

GOD: **Do you feel my presence now?**

JIM: Yes, but I guess I wasn't expecting to feel it this pointedly. We also come to receive inspiration for the coming week.

GOD: **Do you feel inspired now?**

JIM: Yes, I feel very inspired. I feel within me a renewing of my faith. I feel within me . . . .

16

GOD: James! I have a job for you.

JIM: What?

GOD: I said I have a job for you.

JIM: Who, me?

GOD: Yes — You!

JIM: Are you sure?

GOD: Yes.

JIM: Well, OK but maybe you'd better tell me some other time. Right now we have to get on with the service and then I have to get home for dinner and then there is a basketball game on TV this afternoon and then I have a youth meeting tonight and then . . . .

GOD: James. Are you trying to avoid me?

JIM: Well, if you want the truth, I'm not sure I want to know what the job is because I'm not sure I will want to do it.

GOD: I just heard you pray to me, and I quote, "not my will but thine be done." Didn't you mean that?

JIM: I thought I did; at least it sounded good.

GOD: I don't want good sounding words from you. I want you. I want your commitment. I want you to do a job for me.

JIM: But what if I don't want to do it?

GOD: That is your decision. I do not force anyone. I have created you with a free will. You can choose to follow me or you can choose another course for your life.

JIM: I think I'd better listen to what you have to say. Would you mind arranging it so I'm the only one who can hear you?

GOD: All right.
(Silence as Jim's face changes to fear.)

17

JIM: Is that all?

GOD: **Yes.**

JIM: I don't think you have the right person.

GOD: **Do you question my judgment?**

JIM: No, but . . .

GOD: **I have chosen you.**

JIM: But I don't have any talent in that area. Now Dave, he would be a lot better at that. He eats that stuff up.

GOD: **I have given Dave his job, this is for you to do.**

JIM: But what if I make a fool of myself? What if people laugh at me or don't accept me? I couldn't handle that. I would be so embarrassed. If I messed up, people would crucify me. Do you have any idea of what that is like?

GOD: **Yes.**
(Pause)

JIM: Time! What about time? Do you realize how much time that would take? I've got too much to do now. I can't get everything done I'm supposed to do. And now you're trying to load something else on me.

GOD: **Excuses, excuses. You remind me of another man I once had a job for. His name was Moses. His job was a lot bigger than the one I have given to you. He, too, came up with excuses for why he shouldn't do the job. He was afraid he did not have the talent to do the job because of his speech impediment. He also was afraid of not being accepted. *But, he did it anyway.***

JIM: But that was *Moses*. I am just me.

GOD: **You are the one I have chosen.**

JIM: But Moses was just watching some sheep. He had plenty of time. I don't. My life is just full of things to be done.

18

GOD: **Perhaps you need to take some rocks out of your cup.**

JIM: Now wait a minute. That was just a children's sermon. That message was for the children.

GOD: **You are *my* child.**
(Jim picks up cup, plays with rocks.)

JIM: You know, the more I think about it, it doesn't really sound that bad. It would be challenging. It is worthwhile. A lot more worthwhile than some of these rocks I have filling up my life. Do you still promise to be with me?

GOD: **I have said I will be with you always.**

JIM: It's not going to be easy.

GOD: **I didn't say that it would be easy. I said I would be with you.**

JIM: Then let's do it. I'll get rid of some of the rocks and we'll have a go at it. *(To congregation)* Will you join me as I continue to talk to God.
    God, help us to break through the excuses that we set up that keep us from accepting your way in our lives. Amen.

3
"Who Is My Neighbor?"

Luke 10:25–37

(Chancel is set with table, chair, a plant, coffee cup, saucer, and folded newspaper. Jim comes in, pours cup of coffee, sits down, sips coffee, opens newspaper, ignores front section, goes right to the sports page. Comments on the sporting events of the day.)

GOD: May I have the front page, please?

JIM: Sure. *(Absentmindedly holds out the front section, then realizes there is no one there. Looks around in surprise. Lays the paper back down slowly and begins to read again.)*

GOD: May I have the front page, please?

JIM: What? Who is that?

GOD: I am who I am.

JIM: Hello, God.

GOD: Hello, James.

JIM: It has been a while since we talked like this. I still can't get over your being here in my kitchen.

20

GOD: I told you I am with you always, wherever you are.

JIM: Yes, you did. Well, uh . . . how have you been . . . uh . . . how do you like the weath . . . uh . . . What do you want?

GOD: Could I see the front page of the newspaper?

JIM: Why do you want that?

GOD: You don't seem to be using it.

JIM: Well, I was reading the sports page right now.

GOD: Aren't you interested in what is going on in my world?

JIM: Why, yes. Sports are a part of your world.

GOD: Yes, they are and they seem to be a very important part to you.

JIM: Yes, they are. There is nothing wrong with sports, is there?

GOD: No. I like to see my people entertain and enjoy themselves, but you can't let sports be your whole life. There are other things going on in my world that I am concerned about and I want you to be aware of them.

JIM: Oh, I am aware of your world. Remember I have to go out into that world every day with all its pressures and problems. It's not easy, you know. I mean, it wouldn't be so bad if all I had to do was float around on a cloud all day. *(Pause)*

GOD: Is that your concept of me, James?

JIM: No, I didn't mean that. It's just that some days are really frustrating. There is so much work to be done—places to go—people's feelings to be considered—meetings to attend—ideas to be sifted through—demands to be met—conflicts to be solved—sometimes I find myself in situations where I just don't know what to do.

GOD: I have said I will be with you always.

21

JIM: I know, and sometimes I remember that and it really seems to help—the answers come and the road is smoothed, but other times I forget and I feel all alone, like the burden of solving all the problems is on my shoulders. It's mornings like that that all I want to do is to crawl back into bed, pull the covers up over my head and go back to sleep.

GOD: **My son, James, the ostrich.**

JIM: Wait a minute now. I said I feel like pulling the covers up over my head. I didn't say I did it. I get up and get going—get going out into your world.

GOD: **And what do you find there?**

JIM: Well, I find a lot of things.

GOD: **What kinds of things do you find in my world?**

JIM: Well, I find a lot of beauty. Particularly at this time of year with everything turning green and buds starting to pop out. There is the grass and the trees and the freshness of springtime air. Soon there will be flowers and the warmth of the summer sun. Last year I got to spend a week in the Rocky Mountains and they are fantastic! I have seen the beauty and power of waterfalls as well as the beauty and elegance of a butterfly. Your whole creation is so beautiful, so inspiring.

GOD: **I'm glad you approve of my creation. I am disturbed, however, by what all of you are doing to my water-ways and air; but that is a subject for another discussion. Right now I want to get back to your observations of my world. You seem to be only aware of one aspect. You did not even mention the most important part of my creation.**

JIM: I didn't?

GOD: **No, you didn't.**

JIM: Well, I mentioned the trees, grass, flowers, mountains—all of nature, animals—all the different kinds of animals.

GOD: The animals are a wonderful part of creation. They give me very little trouble. But animals are not what I was talking about. What you have left out of my creation is people—my people—my children.

JIM: Oh, I'm aware of people. There are my wife and children, my mother and father and sister—all my relatives. The people I work with, my friends, my neighbors . . . .

GOD: I am concerned about your neighbors.

JIM: Chuck and Marilyn? What's the matter with them? Has something happened?

GOD: No, not Chuck and Marilyn.

JIM: The Pattersons?

GOD: No, not the Pattersons.

JIM: Who then? Tell me.

GOD: John and Trudy Evans.

JIM: Evans? There are no Evanses in my neighborhood.

GOD: The Evanses live in the Homes of Oakridge and they are having a lot of trouble meeting their basic needs.

JIM: Homes of Oakridge? That's not my neighborhood. That's clear down beyond the church.

GOD: Another neighbor of yours I'm concerned about is little Becky Jones.

JIM: There's no Jones in our neighborhood.

GOD: She lives at Woodhaven Learning Center. She struggles to understand even the simplest parts of life.

JIM: I've heard of Woodhaven. It's one of the church's homes for mentally and physically retarded children and adults. But that is way down in Missouri.

GOD: I am also concerned about another neighbor of yours. Manuel Gotez.

JIM: Manuel Gotez? There isn't a Juan in my neighborhood.

GOD: Manuel Gotez is in jail in Paraguay because he tried to form a cooperative farming venture with the people who lived in his village.

JIM: Paraguay? Paraguay?

GOD: Yes, Paraguay.

JIM: Now wait a minute. You said these people were my neighbors, but they don't live close to me at all. They don't live in my neighborhood so they're not my neighbors. Paraguay?

GOD: They are your neighbors.

JIM: They are?

GOD: Yes, James.

JIM: Well, maybe I don't understand what a neighbor is.

GOD: In your mind a neighbor is someone who lives within a few blocks of you. Your problem, James, is that your neighborhood is too small.

JIM: Well, if it's not just those who live around me, who is my neighbor?

GOD: Do you remember the parable of the Good Samaritan?

JIM: Sure I do. It's about this guy who was walking along the road and some robbers beat him up and took his money and left him on the side of the road. Two guys, a priest and a Levite, walked by him on the other side of the road and wouldn't help; but then the Good Samaritan came along and he took the man to an inn and got him fixed up and paid for his food and for a room.

GOD: Do you know why he was called a Samaritan?

24

JIM: Well, I always figured Samaritan meant someone who was willing to help.

GOD: **No, it has come to be synonymous with helper but that is not what it meant. It meant someone who lived in Samaria, as a European lives in Europe.**

JIM: Oh.

GOD: **Do you remember why Jesus told the parable of the Good Samaritan?**

JIM: Sure . . . uh . . . no.

GOD: **A teacher of the Law was trying to trap Jesus and asked him, "What must I do to receive eternal life?" Jesus turned it back to him by asking him what he thought the scriptures said. The man answered, "You must love the Lord your God with all your heart, and with all your soul, and with all your strength, and with all your mind, *and* you must love your neighbor as yourself." Jesus replied, "You are correct. Do this and you will live." But the teacher wasn't through yet. He then asked Jesus, "Who is my neighbor?" The same question you just asked, James. And Jesus told the parable to answer his question. You see, James, the beaten man and the Good Samaritan were neighbors.**

JIM: You mean the beaten man lived in Samaria, too?

GOD: **No, James. What made them neighbors is that one of them was in need and the other cared enough to help.**

JIM: Oh. Then anyone who is in need is my neighbor, and I become a neighbor by caring for and helping others.

GOD: **I believe you're beginning to see the light.**

JIM: And as the scripture says, loving and caring for my neighbor goes right along with loving you.

GOD: **That's right.**

JIM: I guess I have made my neighborhood too small.

GOD: The boundaries of your neighborhood are not made up of streets. The only boundary your neighborhood has is your love for me. The greater your love for me becomes, the larger your neighborhood becomes.

JIM: Then the real way to show my love to you is to be a Good Samaritan—a good neighbor to those in need around me.

GOD: Fine. Now what are we going to do about the Evanses and Becky Jones and Manuel Gotez?

JIM: Who?

GOD: Your neighbors that I mentioned to you earlier.

JIM: But I don't know them.

GOD: You mean they weren't in the sports page today? Excuse me. I just couldn't resist. James, there are a lot of needy people in this world that you don't know.

JIM: Well, how do I go about being a neighbor to them? Even if I am made aware of them I can't be a neighbor to everyone all at the same time. How do I extend myself out?

GOD: Do you want it in one word?

JIM: Sure.

GOD: Stewardship!

JIM: Stewardship?

GOD: You look as if that disturbs you.

JIM: Well, I suppose that's not my favorite word.

GOD: Stewardship is *one* of the *best* ways of being a neighbor. Time and talent are very important in being a neighbor to someone in need. But you are right, you can't personally be a neighbor to everyone all at the same time, so financial stewardship is a way of extending your care and help. As you give to the church, my children—your neighbors here in town, in the United States and around the world are being helped by you. It is the way for you to, as you put it, extend yourself. That is why it is so important for you to begin to think in terms of percentage giving to the church. I understand that your church is having a Day of the Tithe.

JIM: Yes, that's right, this Sunday. I read about that in the church paper. That was set up to help us experience percentage giving. And the money from that is going to be split up between Homes of Oakridge, Woodhaven, and Friendship Mission in Paraguay. Those just happen to be the places you mentioned where my three neighbors live.

GOD: Very perceptive, James. Are you planning on taking a day's tithe to church on Sunday?

JIM: Sure.

GOD: Have you written your check yet?

JIM: Uh.

GOD: Well!
(Jim takes out checkbook and writes check.)

GOD: Very good. That wasn't so hard, was it?

JIM: No. As a matter of fact it felt pretty good to be a neighbor. Well, I better get to work. I'll see you later.

GOD: James, I am with you always.

JIM: Right. You know, God, as we go through this day—I might just see a few neighbors I've never seen before.

4
"I Didn't Mean To"

Romans 7:18–19

(Stage is set with an easy chair and a folding chair. Jim comes in from work, acts very tired, sits down in chair.)

JIM: What a day. *(Stretch — yawn)* I've got an hour before I have to be back at the church for a meeting. Nobody's home. If I can just sit down here, relax and take it easy for a little bit. I'll read the paper. *(Picks up paper, thumbs through, starts to nod, falls asleep. Moment of silence)*

SON: *(Comes bounding on stage — loud voice)* Hey, Dad.

JIM: *(Startled awake)* What's the matter with you, couldn't you see I was resting?

SON: *(Quieted)* I'm sorry, I guess I didn't think.

JIM: You're darn right you didn't think. How many times have I told you to pay attention to what's going on around you? You have got to be more considerate of other people's feelings. You are not the only person in this house.
(Son starts to walk away, dejected.)

JIM: Well, what did you want?

28

SON: I thought we might play some basketball.

JIM: Are you kidding? I just got home from work. I've got just a little time to relax and I'm not going to play basketball.

SON: *(Pauses, looks away, tries one more time)* Do you want to help me fix my bike?

JIM: Can't you understand English? I need some time to relax. Now leave me alone!
(Son walks off stage, dejected. Leaves basketball. Jim shakes head, leans back in chair.)

GOD: I want to talk to you.

JIM: I told you I need . . . . *(realizes no one is there, looks around)* I must have fallen asleep fast. *(Settles back.)*

GOD: I want to talk to you.

JIM: Who is that?

GOD: I am who I am!

JIM: Oh, hello, God.

GOD: Hello, James, I said I want to talk to you.

JIM: I still can't get used to your being here in my house.

GOD: I told you I am with you always.

JIM: I know, I know. You keep saying that, but I don't always remember.

GOD: Now, about what I want to talk about.

JIM: It certainly is nice talking to you, but you kind of caught me at a bad time. I just got home and I've got to be back down at the church in a few minutes for a meeting.

GOD: What kind of meeting?

JIM: It's a Christian Community Living Department meeting.

29

GOD: Is there any chance the Christian Community Living Department will be discussing how parents relate to their children?

JIM: No, see the CCL Department plans ways the members of our church can serve the community. What you're talking about is family relations, and that would probably come under Teaching Ministry although the Membership Department could sponsor a workshop . . . . See, the church structure gets a little complicated sometimes.

GOD: I know.

JIM: But we at First Christian are really trying to understand what it means to be your church, how we can serve each other and our community.

GOD: I understand that, but the church is not what I want to talk to you about today.

JIM: Oh, it's not?

GOD: No, James.

JIM: Well, I don't suppose you want to talk about the weather. Thanksgiving is just over and Christmas is coming. It could be one of those. Although possibly it could be about the youth group at the church, or the women's fellowship, but you said you didn't want to talk about the church. So it couldn't be that. Well then maybe it is about . . . .

GOD: James.

JIM: . . . . about some special project you have for me.

GOD: James! Why don't you just be quiet and let me tell you what I want to talk to you about.

JIM: Oh, quiet. OK I'll be quiet.

GOD: I want to talk about the conversation you just had with your son.

JIM: *(Makes a face of anguish, says under breath)* I was afraid of that. *(Then defensively)* Did you see what he did? Did you hear what he said? He comes bursting in here, disturbs my rest and all he wanted was to play basketball. He is so inconsiderate.

GOD: **Why are you so upset with him?**

JIM: Why am I upset? I just told you. He came bursting in here, disturbed my . . . .

GOD: **James, I repeat. Why are you so upset with him?**

JIM: *(Pause)* I'm not upset with him *(mumbles)* I'm upset with myself.

GOD: **What did you say?**

JIM: I said I am upset with myself.

GOD: **Is that why you have been trying to avoid talking about this?**

JIM: Yes.

GOD: **Why are you upset with yourself?**

JIM: Because he really didn't do anything wrong. I mean—all he wanted to do was play some basketball. That isn't even *really* it. What he *really* wanted was to spend some time with his dad. He just wanted some love and attention. I jumped all over him. I accused him of being selfish and inconsiderate, when all along I knew I was the one who was being selfish and inconsiderate. I laid all my guilt feelings on him.

GOD: **Why do you think you did that?**

JIM: I don't know why. That's the problem. I didn't mean to! But I did it.

GOD: **Well, you have taken an important step admitting it.**

JIM: Well, that's not easy. I knew as soon as you spoke what you wanted to talk about, but I was simply trying to avoid it. It is not a pleasant feeling to admit I have done something so stupid as well as insensitive.

GOD: **You have trouble with that?**

JIM: I sure do. It's like the car accident I had last Monday. There I was driving to work down University Avenue and I saw a friend, so I beeped the horn and waved, and when I turned back, there was the back end of that van staring me in the face and *wham*. I just sat there. I thought, "You've had a wreck. It's your fault—no, wait a minute, it must be someone else's fault. It can't be my fault. It's your fault, you stupid . . . ." I won't bother to tell you what else I called myself.

GOD: **I heard.**

JIM: Oh well, the point is I wanted to blame someone else, or something else, anything so I wouldn't have to accept the responsibility for my own stupid act. I mean— I'm teaching my kids to drive, and here I cause $1,000 damage to our car because of something stupid like not watching the road in front of me.

GOD: **I get the feeling that it wasn't the accident or the damage that upset you so much as it was that you did something stupid.**

JIM: I guess you're right.

GOD: **It's difficult to picture yourself as capable of doing something stupid?**

JIM: Well, I am supposed to be a semi-intelligent human being. I should not be driving down the street waving at someone.

GOD: **No, you shouldn't, but do you think you are perfect?**

JIM: No, I'm certainly not perfect. I just got done telling you about a stupid mistake. I certainly am not perfect.

GOD: **But you think you should be?**

JIM: Well, I hadn't thought about it like that, but it sure upsets me when I make mistakes.

GOD: **Speaking of mistakes, let's see what we can learn from your experience with the car wreck and apply it to your conversation earlier with your son.**

JIM: Well, I don't see what they've got to do with each other.

GOD: **What's the matter, don't you want to talk about it?**

JIM: I told you earlier I was trying to avoid talking about that conversation.

GOD: **Why?**

JIM: Because it was a stupid thing to do.

GOD: **Why?**

JIM: Because it was insensitive. He wanted some attention from me and I wouldn't give it. It was just plain insensitive.

GOD: **And being insensitive doesn't fit the image that you have of yourself?**

JIM: No. I'm a Christian and Christians are not supposed to be insensitive.

GOD: **Christians are supposed to be perfect?**

JIM: Well . . . yes! We are supposed to follow the teachings and way of life of Jesus, and certainly he wasn't insensitive. He taught us to accept your will for our lives. You don't want us to be insensitive do you?

GOD: **No, I don't.**

JIM: Well, now we have reached the crux of the matter. I call myself a Christian, I think of myself as a Christian. Yet I keep on doing unchristian things. I find myself in situations and I know what the right thing to do is, but I go right ahead and do what I know is wrong.

GOD: And that doesn't fit with your image of yourself as a Christian?

JIM: No, and it makes me angry with myself. Why can't I do what I know is right?

GOD: James, you know you are not the only one with this problem. All of my children must struggle with their imperfections. Paul had the same problem. He acknowledged it when he wrote his letter to the Romans. He wrote, "I can will what is right, but I cannot do it. For I do not do the good I want, but the evil I do not want is what I do."

JIM: That's it. That is exactly the problem I have. Paul seemed just as frustrated with it as I am. And Paul was an apostle, a great leader in your church. He must have really been upset with himself when he failed.

GOD: He *did*. But he learned a lesson that you don't seem to have learned yet.

JIM: What is that?

GOD: That I loved him. I love you, too, James.

JIM: Oh, I know you love me, at least when I am doing what you want. It's those times when I do what I know is wrong that bothers me.

GOD: I also love you then.

JIM: You do?

GOD: Yes, James.

JIM: But if those things upset me so much, I would think they must really upset you.

GOD: James, when you fail to live as I would have you live, I am disappointed in you, but I continue to love you and I forgive you when you recognize you're wrong and ask my forgiveness. The problem does not lie with my forgiving you; it lies with your forgiving yourself.

JIM: My forgiving myself?

GOD: **Yes, James, you must recognize that being a Christian does not mean you are perfect. You are a follower of Christ, not Christ himself. Jesus and the life he lived on earth are examples for you. He lived as I would have all my children strive to live. But that striving is a lifelong growing process. It is a path to follow. When you do what you know is wrong, you experience guilt. Some guilt is good for you for it helps you recognize that you have turned off that path. But do not allow your guilt to become like quicksand, pulling you down and down. Instead, forgive yourself, as I have forgiven you, and use your guilt as a guidepost to get you back onto the path that we both would have you travel. Learn from your mistakes and do not seek to be Christ, but to be more Christlike. You are one of my children, James, and I love you.**

JIM: Thank you. I will try to love myself enough to forgive myself and to use my guilt to keep me on that path. *(Checks watch)* Uh, God, I have a *few* minutes before I have to go. It's been nice talking to you, but there is something I really *want* to do now. So if you're finished I need to go outside. See you later.

GOD: **James, you are talking again as if you are leaving me here. I have told you I am with you always.**

JIM: Oh, yes, that's right. Well, how would you like to referee a quick basketball game?

5

"Am I Successful?"

Luke 19:1–10

(In the chancel is a table with tablecloth, two cups of coffee, newspaper. Pat seated at table. Jim rushes in, checks watch, in a real hurry, pours a cup of coffee, picks up paper, sits down, checks watch, stands up, never looks at Pat, makes a couple of comments about all the important things he has to do today.)

JIM: I've got to hurry. Got to get to the church. I've two big meetings that are really important to the future of the church. If I can just convince the people. Why does everything depend on me? *(takes sip of coffee, continues to look at paper, checks watch)* I've got to go. *(Puts down paper, takes a last sip, gives a kiss in the general direction of Pat's cheek. Goes out a make-believe door at front of chancel and starts down the stairs.)*

GOD: James.

JIM: *(Stops, looks around. Starts off again.)*

GOD: James.

JIM: Who is that? *(Pat leaves.)*

GOD: I am who I am.

36

JIM: What?

GOD: I said, "I am who I am."

JIM: Oh, hello, God.

GOD: Hello, James. It has been almost a year since we had a little chat.

JIM: I know it has. Where have you been? Do you have any idea of what has been going on at the church in the past year?

GOD: Yes, James, I know. I want to talk with you.

JIM: Well, after a year, you picked a bad time. I've got two meetings this morning that are vitally important and a thousand other things to do.

GOD: I said I want to talk, now.

JIM: But I told you, I've got to go to the meetings. Don't you care about my church?

GOD: Yes, James, I care about *my* church. *(pause)* But right now I am concerned about you.

JIM: OK. What do you want to talk about?

GOD: Who was that person at your kitchen table?

JIM: Well, that was Pat.

GOD: How do you know?

JIM: Because she's always at the table in the morning. *(pause)* I mean because I just talked with her. That's how I know.

GOD: Oh. You talked with her?

JIM: Yes.

GOD: What did she have to say?

JIM: Well, she said . . . *(pause)* Well, she doesn't talk a lot in the morning.

GOD: **I think I understand why, James. I want you to go back inside.**

JIM: What? I told you I'm in a hurry. I've got two meetings . . . .

GOD: **James!**

JIM: *(Goes back on chancel, acts like he is holding the door open for God)*

GOD: **I'm in here.**

JIM: *(Enters)* She's not here.

GOD: **That's OK. Now sit down. I want to talk to you.**

JIM: *(Jim sits very stiff and tense, checks watch.)* OK. I'm ready.

GOD: **Now take your shoes off.**

JIM: What?

GOD: **I said, take your shoes off.**

JIM: *(Reluctantly takes shoes off.)*

GOD: **Now lean back and put your feet up on the table.**

JIM: On the kitchen table?

GOD: **Lean back and put your feet up on the table!**

JIM: *(Does so.)*

GOD: **Close your eyes.** *(Pause)* **Now take a deep breath.**

JIM: *(Takes a quick, loud breath.)*

GOD: **Take a *slow* deep breath.** *(Pause)* **Now another.** *(Pause)* **You sure have a difficult time relaxing, don't you?**

JIM: Well, if a person is going to be successful he doesn't have time to relax.

GOD: **That, James, is what I want to talk to you about—your concept of what it means to be successful.**

JIM: What's wrong with my concept of success?

GOD: **What makes you think there is something wrong with your concept?**

JIM: Well, usually when you decide it's time for us to have one of these little chats you have a rather pointed lesson for me.

GOD: **That's true. Tell me, James, are you successful?**

JIM: Am I successful?

GOD: **Yes, are you successful?**

JIM: Well, I think I am doing pretty well. I have a good job that provides a decent standard of living—not so high as some, but better than others. We have a nice, comfortable home to live in—not so nice as some, but a lot better than many others. We have two cars—they're not brand new, but they make a nice appearance. I'm able to afford some nice clothes. I mean—I don't buy them at Nieman-Marcus, but I don't get them at Goodwill either.

GOD: **But are you successful?**

JIM: That's what I'm telling you.

GOD: **You've told me what you have, but you haven't told me if you are successful.**

JIM: I think most people look at their possessions to determine how successful they are. There are other status symbols, such as living in the right neighborhood, liking the right kind of food, drinking the right kind of wine, having a big office with a good view. You know, the old key to the executive washroom syndrome. I think even in this day of women's liberation there are many wives who determine their own success through the success of their husbands.

The wife of the president of the company feels more important than the wife of the delivery man. Success is a vertical concept. You rise to success. You come up in the world. You work, struggle, and battle your way to the top. You're either in high society or you're low man on the totem pole. We spend our whole lives trying to get to the top.

GOD: **For those who get there, do they find it worth the effort?**

JIM: Well, there are lots of rewards, the finances and all the comforts they can buy, status, power, influence; but there is also the pressure that comes with success, the pressure of staying at the top, of continuing to excel. There is always someone else who would like to have your job; the pressure of maintaining your standard of living that you have become used to; the pressure of demands upon your time and the pressure of always having to make the right decisions. I guess ulcers are often a reward of success.

GOD: **Why do people work so hard to get ulcers?**

JIM: We don't try to get ulcers; they are just a byproduct of our striving for success. Achieving success is how we feel important. It is what makes us worth something. It makes us winners.

GOD: **Winning seems to be very important.**

JIM: No one wants to be a loser.

GOD: **I know. You should have heard the number of prayers that came to me from athletic teams this past week.**

JIM: Winning is important. It makes you feel good. You're better than the other person or team. Like in tennis. Sometimes when I'm playing tennis, I really get into it. I mean I just drive myself. Nothing else matters!

GOD: **I know, James. I have heard some of your comments when you make a bad shot.**

JIM: Oh. Well, winning is important. That's how we build our self-esteem. I mean, winners are winners and losers are losers. Life is like a game and you've got to beat the other people so you can win. Vince Lombardi summed it up when he said, "Winning isn't everything. It is the only thing."

GOD: **Vince Lombardi was wrong and you are wrong, James.** *(Pause, let the words sink in.)* **Think back to when we started this conversation. You were in such a hurry that you didn't even take time to acknowledge your wife's presence. When is the last time you have spent an evening just with her or gone away for a weekend, just the two of you? When is the last time you spent some real time with your kids? When is the last time you really relaxed? Even when you play tennis you get so upset with yourself for not playing as well as you think you should that you just end up frustrated. You're running here and there, placing unreasonable demands upon yourself, letting other people place demands upon you. You're living in a pressure cooker, you're getting nervous, your hair is turning gray, when your stomach isn't churning—it's tied up in knots. Is this really enjoying life, the life I have given you? I have heard you in prayers thank me for the gift of life. Why would you thank me for the life you are living?**

JIM: What am I supposed to do, chuck it all, quit my job and go off and be a hermit?

GOD: **No, James, you don't need to chuck it all. What you need to do is look at your goals.**

JIM: My goals?

GOD: **Yes, your goals. Your goals seem to be status, prestige, power and influence. Why do you have those goals?**

JIM: I want to be successful.

GOD: **James, you achieve success by accomplishing your goals. I asked, why are those your goals?**

JIM: Society has always taught me to strive after those goals. That's what makes me worthwhile.

GOD: We will deal with what makes you worthwhile in a minute. If you accept the goals that society has taught you, does that make you a societian?

JIM: A what?

GOD: A societian—someone who believes in and follows the teachings of society.

JIM: No, I'm a Christian. I follow the teachings of Jesus.

GOD: Do you? Are those goals the goals that Jesus taught?

JIM: *(Pause)* No.

GOD: What would you say are the goals that Jesus taught?

JIM: I suppose it can be summed up in the two commandments— to love you and to love our neighbors. But I do love you and I do make an effort to love my neighbors.

GOD: Yes, there are times you do. Did you express your love to your wife a few minutes ago?

JIM: No, why do I do that?

GOD: Because you let your other goals take precedence over your Christian goals. You simply need to get those in perspective. You're not the only one who does this. I have heard people say, "In this profession you've got to climb over some people if you want to get to the top." It is not whether you get to the top that is important. It is how you relate to people enroute.

JIM: You're saying that what I've got to do is keep my goals in perspective. That if one of my other goals comes in conflict with my Christian goals, then I'd better strive to be a success as a Christian.

GOD: That's right. Now on the matter of self-worth. Your worth as a person is not determined by the size of your house, how many cars you have, the importance of your job, or even by whom you can beat in tennis. Your worth is derived by the fact that you are one of my children. **All children of mine have an inherent worth. Their worth is maintained by keeping their goals in perspective, by living up to their potential as one of my children, the potential shown to them by Jesus.**

JIM: Well, this certainly has given me a lot to work on.

GOD: **Yes, it has. I hope the next time I hear you thank me for the gift of life that I will be able to understand why.**

JIM: So do I. So do I. Well, before I go off to work, I think I'll go say good-by to Pat. See you later.

GOD: **James, remember I am with you always.**

JIM: Right. I'll remember.

6

"The Church in Your Life"

1 Corinthians 12:4–7,25–27

(Jim is at a desk in the middle of the chancel. He is attempting to write a stewardship sermon and is becoming very frustrated.)

JIM: I know times are tough, so whatever you can give to the church will be appreciated. *(pause)* No, that's too wishy-washy. *(Crumples up paper. Begins writing again.)* If you don't give to the church, you are going to go to . . . . No, I don't think I want to say that. *(Crumples up paper. Thinks. Starts writing again.)* Money is the root of all evil! No, that's not even true. *(Crumples up paper. Looks off into space. Starts singing)* Money, Money, Money *(pause)* Praise to the money *(pause)* My faith looks up to money . . . . I hate to write stewardship sermons. God, I hate it!

GOD: Hello, James.

JIM: *(Picks up telephone absentmindedly)* Hello *(Looks at phone. Puts it back. Goes back to work.)*

GOD: Hello, James.

JIM: Who is that?

GOD: I am who I am.

44

JIM: What?

GOD: I said, "I am who I am."

JIM: Oh, hello, God.

GOD: Hello, James. We haven't had a little chat since October.

JIM: I know we haven't. Do you have any idea what has been happening at the church since October?

GOD: Yes, I know. I want to talk with you.

JIM: Well, you picked a bad time. I have got to get this sermon done. Couldn't we talk later?

GOD: I said I want to talk with you—now!

JIM: But I said I've got to get this sermon done. Don't you care if I get it done?

GOD: Yes, James, I care if you get it done, but I care more about what you say in it.

JIM: But that's the trouble, I don't know what to say.

GOD: I noticed you were having some trouble. I hope you weren't planning on singing those songs Sunday.

JIM: Oh, no! I haven't begun to worship money, not yet anyway.

GOD: What do you mean "not yet"?

JIM: Well, sometimes I worry about myself. Money seems to be coming more and more important to me.

GOD: Tell me about it.

JIM: Well, I know that in the Bible it says you will take care of our every need just like you take care of the birds and flowers, but you seem to have given me the responsibility of taking care of a lot of our needs. The more money I make the more needs there seem to be. I don't have any more in the bank now than when we were first married, and the bills just keep rolling in. Pat's in college. Kent starts college this fall and Connie will start in two years. We had to buy a new car. There are orthodontist bills, the Sears bill, insurance bills and Iowa Power, and they're just the big things. Most of the time it's the little things that kill your budget.

GOD: It sounds as if you really feel poor.

JIM: Oh, don't get me wrong. I know I'm not poor. I know I am much better off than the vast majority of the people in this world and a lot of the people in our church. It's not just me. It's everybody. In this day of inflation and interest rates the way they are, we are all feeling the squeeze, and for some it's more like a crunch. Now, this Sunday, I have to get up in front of all those people and give a stewardship sermon. I have to convince them that they ought to be giving more money to the church. Sometimes I feel like a TV celebrity, but instead of selling dog food or soap, I'm supposed to sell the church. I'm supposed to tell the people how much the church needs their money and convince them to give. How can I do that?

GOD: You can't.

JIM: I've got to convince . . . . What?

GOD: I said, you can't.

JIM: What do you mean I can't? I've got to. Do you know the financial situation at the church?

GOD: Yes, I know.

JIM: Well, then you know how important it is that we increase our pledges this year. We have the opportunity really to grow, to move ahead in our ministry, to expand our programs and services. That takes time involvement on the part of the people, but it also takes staff and the upkeep of facilities. It takes materials and heat and electricity. We also have to support the larger work of the church through our outreach giving. When it comes right down to it, it takes money. If I don't convince the people to increase their pledges this year, then we are going to have to cut back drastically and once a church starts cutting back it starts to die. I don't want this church to die. I have got to convince the people to give more.

GOD: **You can't.**

JIM: What do you mean, I can't? I've got to.

GOD: **What I mean is that you cannot convince people to give more. In fact, that is not even what I want you to try to do.**

JIM: It's not?

GOD: **No, it is not.**

JIM: Well, what am I supposed to do in the sermon?

GOD: **I'm glad you *finally* are considering what *I* want as you prepare a sermon . . . but let's leave that for a few minutes. Let's talk about money first.**

JIM: What about it?

GOD: **What is money to you?**

JIM: Well, I guess money basically is what we use for a means of exchange. We take our money and exchange it for housing, food, services, travel and entertainment.

GOD: **That's fine. What else is it?**

JIM: Some people use it as a status symbol, kind of like a barometer to measure their own self worth. The more money they have the more important they feel.

GOD: **I did *not* intend money to be used that way. A person's worth is not based on how much money he or she has. A person's worth is derived from the fact that he or she is one of my children.**

JIM: I know that. In fact, as I remember it, that was the subject of our last chat. All I'm trying to do is tell you how we human beings view money.

GOD: Go on.

JIM: Some people try to use money to buy happiness and friends. They think if they buy enough things people will like them, and if they get people to like them, even on that basis, they will be happy. It's kind of like the prodigal son. In the story of the prodigal son this younger brother asks the father for his inheritance and then . . . .

GOD: James.

JIM: Yes?

GOD: I *am familiar* with the story!

JIM: Oh, that's right. I guess you would be. Well, there is something else money is used for and that is power and influence. Some people try to use their money so that they can get their way and get special privileges.

GOD: That also is not what I intended money to be used for. To help you understand money a little better perhaps I need to take you back a step further. Tell me, those people you will be talking to Sunday, how do they get their money?

JIM: They work for it or have worked for it and now get social security.

GOD: That's right. Money becomes important to them because they have invested themselves in it. They have invested their time, effort and ingenuity. In return for this investment they receive compensation—wages or salary—in the form of money. That check may represent hard manual labor, hours of pulling a lever on an assembly line, creative energy spent in trying to come up with a new idea or design, healing a sick person or stimulating a child's mind. Whatever the nature of the work, a big portion of themselves went into it. Therefore, a portion of themselves is invested in government when they pay taxes, a portion of themselves goes into the cash register at the grocery store, a portion of themselves goes off to college with their children, a portion of themselves is lost when they squander money on something foolish, and a portion of themselves is included in their gift to the church.

48

JIM: I think I'm beginning to understand. Because we have invested so much of ourselves in making the money, it then becomes very important what we do with it.

GOD: **That's absolutely right.**

JIM: Well, how does all that apply to the church?

GOD: **For years, churches and ministers have been trying to *convince* people to give to the church. They have tried all different kinds of methods. They have tried brow-beating, they have tried making them feel guilty, they have tried calling their Christian commitment into question, they have tried threatening them. There have been as many bad methods used as there are bad concepts of the use of money that we talked about.**

JIM: But the church has to have money.

GOD: **That's right.**

JIM: And that money has to come from the people.

GOD: **Correct.**

JIM: Well, then?

GOD: **Well then, what?**

JIM: Why do the people give?

GOD: **The people give to the church when the church is being the church.**

JIM: I don't understand.

GOD: **A little while ago you started to quote the prodigal son to me. Let me quote a piece of scripture to you. It comes from Paul's first letter to my children at Corinth. "And so there is no division in the body, but all its different parts have the same concern for one another. If one part of the body suffers, all the other parts suffer with it; if one part is praised, all the other parts share its happiness. All of you, then, are Christ's body, and each one is a part of it."**

49

JIM: What does that scripture have to do with stewardship? I mean, I could understand if you had quoted about the widow and the two mites or the rich young ruler, but why that one?

GOD: Because that scripture talks about the church. That scripture tells how to go about *being* the church. I mean the body of my Son on earth. The church as I want it to be. The church that is alive and vital. The church that is touching people's lives, healing hurts and ministering to needs. The church where the people see themselves as an important part of that body. The church where people can *invest* themselves in something their faith tells them is worthwhile.

JIM: Let me see if I can put this all together. Our money is important to us because we have invested so much of ourselves to earn it. Therefore we will invest it where we decide it is worthwhile to invest ourselves, and that will be the church if the church is truly being the church as you want it to be.

GOD: You're coming right along, James. You are not going to convince the people to give because of one sermon. That is a long-range growth process. At this point they either feel they are a vital part of Christ's body or they don't. They either feel the work and ministry is worthwhile enough to invest themselves and their money or they don't. Either they feel the church is *vital* in their life or they don't.

JIM: But I still have to preach a sermon Sunday.

GOD: Yes, you do.

JIM: Would it be OK if I used that scripture you quoted?

GOD: It is part of my word.

JIM: And for a title I could use that line you just said, "The Church in Your Life."

GOD: That's fine.

50

JIM: Well, I've got the scripture and a title but what do I say?

GOD: **Just tell them what I have told you. Wait a minute. You ministers think every sermon has to have three points to it. Here they are. Are you ready?**

JIM: Yes.

GOD: **First, tell them that I love them. Second, tell them that they are my people and I am their God. Third, tell them that if this church is really striving to be the church, if it is touching people's lives and sharing my love, if the church is truly vital in their lives, then I can think of no better place to invest themselves.**

JIM: Is that it?

GOD: **That's it.**

JIM: OK. I'll tell them. Will you be there Sunday?

GOD: **James, remember I am with you always.**

JIM: I'll remember.

7

"It's Not So Bad"

John 10:10

(Chancel is set as a kitchen with table, chair, cup, newspaper. Jim walks in, looks tired, acts despondent, pours cup of coffee, sits down. Sits dejectedly for a while.)

JIM: Life is the pits. *(Pause)* I don't know what's wrong with me. I feel so . . . so down all the time. Sometimes life doesn't seem worth living. *(Picks up newspaper.)* This is depressing. Look at all these people with problems. Nothing seems to be going right these days. *God, life is the pits!*

GOD: Hello, James. *(Jim looks around.)* **Hello, James.**

JIM: Who is that?

GOD: I am who I am.

JIM: *(Despondently.)* Oh, hello, God.

GOD: I want to talk to you.

JIM: Sure, God, whatever you say.

GOD: Well, this is unusual. Usually when I want to talk to you, you have all kinds of excuses of why you are too busy to talk.

JIM: Well, let's see. We haven't talked since last spring. I figured you didn't care anymore.

GOD: I care, James.

JIM: Well, if you cared, I figure you would come around more.

GOD: James, I have told you, "I am with you always."

JIM: Yes, I know. But sometimes it is hard to remember.

GOD: I've noticed. But right now let's talk about life.

JIM: Oh, that should be a thrilling subject.

GOD: I would hope that it would be, but somehow I get the feeling you're not too excited. I don't believe I have ever seen you down like this before.

JIM: I can't remember ever feeling like this before.

GOD: Life really has you down?

JIM: It seems so. Nothing seems to be going right for me.

GOD: You know, for not having much experience, you are really pretty good at this.

JIM: Pretty good at what?

GOD: Self-pity.

JIM: What do you mean self-pity? I'm not engaging in self-pity. I just think life is the pits. It's a bummer. I can't get myself going. Everything seems to be coming down around me. I feel down. I feel defeated. I feel useless. I feel alone. I feel ... sorry for myself. Is feeling sorry for yourself anything like self-pity?

GOD: Yes, James.

JIM: Well, maybe I have reason to feel sorry for myself and I'm not the only one feeling like this. I think lots of people are feeling depressed.

GOD: **What do you see as the problems?**

JIM: Well, the economy is one problem. People today are really having a hard time stretching the dollar. Inflation hits everybody hard, and then we are facing gigantic increases in utility costs all the time.

GOD: **People worry a lot about money, don't they?**

JIM: Yes, they do. It is difficult to maintain our standard of living with inflation going the way it is.

GOD: **When you say the standard of living, are you referring to the standard of living in the United States or the standard of living in Europe or the standard of living in Latin America or the standard of living in Uganda or Pakistan?**

JIM: Well, I guess I was referring to the standard of living in the United States.

GOD: **Do you go to bed hungry?**

JIM: No. Not unless I'm on a diet because I've gained too much weight.

GOD: **Do you have a house to live in?**

JIM: Yes, but if I had the money I could buy some new drapes for our bedroom.

GOD: **Do you have clothes to keep you warm?**

JIM: Yes, but if I had the money, there is this sports coat . . . .

GOD: **James, I have too many children in this world without food, without shelter, without clothes to be worrying about a sports coat. If you are going to be depressed because you have to live with some old drapes in your bedroom, then so be it. I can't help you on that one. What else is bothering people?**

54

JIM: Well, I think a lot of people feel lonely.

GOD: **Do you feel lonely?**

JIM: Sometimes.

GOD: **But you have people around you all the time.**

JIM: I know; that's why I don't understand why I get these feelings of loneliness at times. But sometimes I just feel all alone, as if no one else can quite understand what I'm feeling or what I'm going through.

GOD: **What else are you feeling?**

JIM: Pressure. Stress or whatever you want to call it. There just seems to be so much to do and so little time to do it in. Sometimes it can become so overwhelming that all I want to do is chuck the whole thing and run away and hide.

GOD: **Go on.**

JIM: So much of life seems to have no direction or purpose. I move from one thing to another, one day to another, one month to another and here it is, another birthday rolls around and I wonder what I've accomplished in the past year that was worth anything.

GOD: **It sounds as if you and a lot of people are hurting.**

JIM: That's why I say life is the pits.

GOD: **It doesn't have to be.**

JIM: What?

GOD: **I said, it doesn't have to be.**

JIM: What do you mean?

GOD: **Life can be abundant.**

JIM: Are we back to talking about what money can buy?

GOD: No, James. I'm not talking about money. I'm talking about life. Life in all its fullness. Life with purpose and direction. Life as I created it to be. Jesus said, "I have come that you might have life and have it abundantly." That is the kind of life you can have. That is the kind of life everyone can have. The abundant life. That is the kind of life I want you to have.

JIM: But how? That is the queston, how?

GOD: **Are you sure you really want to know?**

JIM: Are you kidding? Of course I want to know. Anything is better than what I've been going through. Why do you even have to ask?

GOD: **Because it means you will have to stop playing this "Oh, woe is me" game. I've noticed a lot of people seem to enjoy the game. They use it to get attention and sympathy.**

JIM: But that is just a sign of how lonely they are.

GOD: **That's right. But the game doesn't work. As long as you keep playing it you will continue to wallow in your own self-pity. Are you really ready to give up the security of that game and take a chance on a different approach to handling your problems?**

JIM: I guess so. I'm willing to give it a try.

GOD: **That's not good enough, James. I don't work on a trial basis. Are you ready or aren't you? I don't force anyone. If you like your life the way it is, then keep it that way. If you want something better, if you want to live the abundant life, then say so. The decision is yours.**

JIM: OK. I'm ready to give up the game of "Oh, woe is me." It's a depressing game anyway. I'm ready to start. What's next?

GOD: **Start talking to me.**

JIM: I'm talking to you right now.

GOD: I don't mean just when I talk to you. I mean talk to me on a regular basis.

JIM: Is this one of those pitches again for daily devotions or a daily time for prayer? That seems so hokey. I mean, I'm a Christian, but I'm not a fanatic.

GOD: You don't have to be a fanatic to talk to me. Look, I am your God and you are one of my people. I made you to be in relationship with me. When you are not in relationship with me you are out of whack with the rest of life. You know that no relationship, marriage or otherwise, can stay on a good, solid basis without good communication. What makes you think our relationship can be solid unless you talk to me regularly?

JIM: But what do I say? It's so hard to choose the proper words.

GOD: I am so tired of being talked to properly and piously. I am your God, your heavenly Father, not some boss who is going to fire you if you say the wrong thing. I love you! I want you just to share your thoughts, your joys, your fears, your feelings with me just as you did a little while ago.

JIM: OK. So I am to pray, talk, communicate, or whatever with you on a regular basis. I am to be in relationship with you and that will give me the abundant life?

GOD: No, that's just the beginning. Next I want you to do something for yourself.

JIM: What?

GOD: It doesn't matter.

JIM: What do you mean?

GOD: Give yourself a present.

JIM: Give myself a present? Buy myself something?

GOD: You could buy yourself something or you could give yourself other kinds of presents such as taking a couple of hours to play tennis or staying home one night and not feeling guilty because you aren't at a meeting or making calls, or take Pat out to dinner and a show just because you want to.

JIM: I remember, as a kid, people used to joke about women—when they would feel down they would go buy themselves a new hat. Is that what you mean?

GOD: Well, that particular example is a stereotype that belongs more in Dagwood and Blondie than in real life, but the principle is the same. You must feel you are worthwhile. You are important. Important enough to give yourself a gift.

JIM: OK. Step two. I'm to do something just for myself because I am worth it. What's next?

GOD: Do something for someone else.

JIM: But it is me that we are trying to teach how to have the abundant life. What does doing something for someone else have to do with it?

GOD: Let's think back to this period of time when you were feeling so down. Did you ever wish someone would do something for you?

JIM: Yes, I can remember thinking to myself that Pat ought to recognize how down I am and do something special for me. I mean, if she really loved me she would do something to make me happy.

GOD: Did she ever do anything?

JIM: Yes.

GOD: How did you feel?

JIM: Well, I felt good, better . . . for a little while. Then I wanted her to do something else to make me happy.

58

GOD: OK, now try to think of a time when you did something for someone else.

JIM: OK. I've got it.

GOD: How did you feel?

JIM: Great. I can still remember that smile of appreciation . . . . I think I'm beginning to get your point. If we are being self-centered in thinking someone else can give us the abundant life, it will never happen. It is when we give of ourselves to others that we find the real joy of living that Jesus always talked about.

GOD: That's why Jesus spent so much time talking about how you should be caring for others.

JIM: Step three. Do something for someone else.

GOD: Now for the fourth and final step. You need a purpose and some goals for your life. What you said earlier about going from day to day, week to week and so on, without ever feeling as if you know where you are going or where you are when you get there, is true for a lot of people.

JIM: I once saw a poster that said, "If you don't know where you are going, you will probably end up someplace else."

GOD: Precisely. A purpose and some goals can make all the difference in your life.

JIM: I remember when I first went to college. I just made mediocre grades, but once I made the decision to go into the ministry and went back to college, I got almost all A's and it was because I had a purpose.

GOD: That's right. A lot of college students hate to see an older person come into class on the first day because they know that person will mess up the grade curve. But the point is no matter what your age, you must set a direction, a purpose for your life, and then set some goals to take you in that direction. Reaching those goals gives you a sense of accomplishment and keeps you moving on toward that abundant life.

59

JIM: Well, now let me see if I have these steps straight.
1. Spend regular time communicating with you.
2. Do something for myself.
3. Do something for someone else.
4. Have a purpose in life with some goals.
Hey, I feel better already.

GOD: **That's good, James, but don't let this quick good feeling lull you into thinking you don't have to work hard at all those steps or you'll be right back in the shape you were in in no time.**

JIM: You know, maybe life isn't so bad after all. I think there is a chance for me, a chance to live the abundant life. OK. Well, I'd better get to work. It's been great talking to you. I'll see you again sometime.

GOD: **James, I have said I am with you always.**

JIM: Right. I'll talk to you again.

GOD: **On a regular basis.**

JIM: Oh, yes. Step one.

8

"I'm Not Through Yet"

Genesis 1:1,26–31

(The chancel is set with the breakfast table, chair, cup, newspaper. Jim walks in, pours a cup of coffee, sits down, picks up the newspaper.)

JIM: This is it. This has got to be it. The end of the world is at hand. All you've got to do is look around. There is trouble everywhere. The whole world is going to pot. Any day now, God is going to say, "That's it! I've had it," and he is just going to destroy the whole world and start over. Well, what are you waiting for, God? If you're going to do it, why don't you go ahead and get it over with! *(Pause)*

GOD: Hello, James. *(Jim looks around)*

GOD: Hello, James.

JIM: Who is that?

GOD: I am who I am.

JIM: Oh, hello, God. God? Hey I wasn't serious. Wait a minute. I'm not ready for the end of the world yet. I've got some things to do. Pat and the kids aren't here.

GOD: James, will you settle down?

JIM: But I really wasn't serious.

GOD: I know. You would be surprised how many things are said using my name about which people are not really serious. Some people ask me to stop them from drinking or smoking or eating too much or even from losing their temper, but they are not serious enough about it to do anything about it themselves. They think I'm the big magic wand in the sky that can cure all their faults and problems without any effort on their part.

JIM: But why don't you do it for them?

GOD: I don't work that way. If they are serious about it, then we can work together, but I don't do those things for people. Now what's this about the end of the world?

JIM: Well, it just seemed to me that you might be about ready to destroy it all.

GOD: Why would I do that? I just created it.

JIM: What do you mean "just created it"? The earth has been around for thousands and thousands of years.

GOD: Are you trying to give me a history lesson, James?

JIM: Well, no . . . but it has been.

GOD: Yes, James, I know. I was there when it was created. It all depends on whose perspective you're looking as to how long it has been. From your perspective it has been a long time. From mine, it hasn't been so long.

JIM: While we are talking about your creating the world, there is a lot of discussion going on about *how* you created it.

GOD: Why is there so much discussion? You can find the truth in Genesis.

JIM: Do you mean that one day you went zap and there was the sun and then another day you went zap and there was the earth and another day you went zap and there were the animals and so on? Some people think that you took thousands of years and created the world through the process of evolution. Now which is true?

GOD: **Does it make any difference?**

JIM: Of course.

GOD: **What difference does it make?**

JIM: Well . . . we would like to know if the Bible is true.

GOD: **I have told you that you can find the truth in Genesis. Now how does Genesis begin?**

JIM: "In the beginning God created the heavens and the earth."

GOD: **There, I told you that you would find the truth. That is all that you need to know. In the beginning I created! How I did it is of no importance to you. The important fact is that I created the world and I created you to live in it.**

JIM: That's another thing that people argue about. Did I really descend from a monkey?

GOD: **Here you are again worrying about how I created. Again you can find all the truth you need in Genesis. I created man in my own image; male and female I created them.**

JIM: But how could you create a female in your image? I mean you are male, aren't you? We do call you father. We make jokes about it. There is the story of the man who met a friend walking down the street and the friend really looked shook up. The man asked the friend what was wrong. The friend said, "I just saw God." The man said, "So?" and the friend said, "She was black!"

GOD: **You could say that I was female and black or you could say I was male and white or red or yellow, for** that matter; but it would be more accurate to say that I am none of those. You see, you continue to misread the scripture of Genesis. You think it says that I was created in the image of man. You continue to try to think of me in human terms. You try to give me human traits. You draw pictures of me and make me an old man with a long robe and a beard. The scripture says that I made you in my image. I am a spirit, a soul, a being, whatever the word you choose to use, and I have created you in that image. Your inner being, the very essence of who you are is made in my image and we relate on that basis. So whether you are male or female or tall or short or fat or skinny or black, white, yellow, red or brown, you are one of my creations created in my image and I seek to be in relationship to you. Do you understand?

JIM: Yes, sir . . . err . . . . Yes, Ma'am . . . err yes, God.

GOD: I think you have a way to go yet, James. But let's get back to this idea about my destroying the world. Why would I want to destroy something I created?

JIM: Well, things do not seem to be going that well. I mean there are trouble and sin all over the place. There is killing in Ireland, rioting in England, bombing in Israel and Lebanon. People all around the world live under oppressive governments in hunger and poverty. Here in the United States things aren't much better. The crime rate is up and the poor are having an even more difficult time surviving. The unemployment rate is high. Things are a mess. It just seems to me that you are apt to be fed up with us and destroy the whole thing.

GOD: I love you.

JIM: What?

GOD: I said, I love you and I love my world. I am not about to destroy you or my world. You see, I'm not through yet! I haven't given up and I don't want you to give up. What are you doing to help the situation?

JIM: Me? What about you? If you're not through yet, if you haven't given up yet then why don't you do something?

64

GOD: I am.

JIM: What?

GOD: I'm talking to you.

JIM: Big deal! I mean—don't get me wrong. I always enjoy these talks, but what good is it going to do to talk to me? What do I have to do with it?

GOD: What else can you remember about that first chapter of Genesis? What responsibilities did I give to the human beings?

JIM: Um . . . to be fruitful and multiply. We certainly have done well on that one.

GOD: True! Too well in some parts of the world. What else?

JIM: Um . . . We were to have dominion over everything.

GOD: And what does dominion mean to you?

JIM: Well, I have always thought it to mean control, authority, or domination.

GOD: Yes, it means that, but I would add one other word.

JIM: What is that?

GOD: Responsibility. When I gave you dominion over the world I also gave you responsibility for it as well.

JIM: Do you mean I'm responsible for the world by myself?

GOD: No, not all by yourself—in partnership with your fellow human beings and with me. You see, James, those things you listed a while ago of what is wrong in the world are true and I am deeply aware of them; however, there is much going on in the world that you did not list. There is an old man who goes into a child care center and sings with the children. They get to experience his love and he experiences theirs. There is a teenage boy who mows the grass for an elderly couple down the street so they won't have to get out in the hot sun. There is a woman who visits regularly in a nursing home to share a little bit of life with the friends she has made there. There is a teenage girl who volunteers at a mentally handicapped school because she cares about their lives. The list goes on and on.

No, James, I haven't given up because I still have millions of partners all over the world who are working with me to make this world what it can be. And that brings us back to you. You have a responsibility. That is a given. That is the way I created this world and you. If you give up, then I have one less partner with whom to work. And the world is that much poorer. I need you to be in partnership with me.

JIM: I guess I never thought of it like that before. I have a responsibility to be in partnership with my fellow human beings and with you to continue the creation process that you started, until this world is like what you want it to be.

GOD: **That's right.**

JIM: And if you haven't given up on it because you love me and this world, then there isn't any reason for me to give up.

GOD: **Perfect, James. You have made some progress.**

JIM: Well, what specifically should I be doing?

GOD: **You will find your way to help if you are truly looking for it. You have many options open to you. Which one you choose isn't as important as the fact that once again you're involved.**

JIM: Well, every time we have one of these little talks you give me an awful lot to think about.

GOD: **And to do.**

JIM: Right. Well, I do appreciate it. I guess I'd better get to work. I'll see you again sometime.

GOD: **James, I have said I am with you always.**

JIM: Oh, that's right . . . partner.

9
"Shalom"

Mark 4:35–40

(Jim comes out and sits down at his desk.)

PERSON REPRESENTING JOB PRESSURE: *(Comes up on the chancel, picks up microphone.)*
Jim, I need to talk to you about the meeting tonight. I know you're busy, but this meeting is really important. It is important to the whole future of the church. After all, you are the senior minister. Those people are counting on you. You've got to think of them and their needs. They are counting on you!
(Lays down the microphone. Walks to the side of the chancel, stops with back to Jim.)

MOTHER: *(Comes to chancel, picks up microphone.)*
You never seem to have any time for me anymore, Jimmy. After all I am your mother. Remember all the times that I took care of you. I always had time for you. That's because you were important to me. Aren't I important to you? Why don't you come by and see me tonight for a little while? I won't keep you long. OK, Jimmy? Tonight, just for a little while? It's important. I'm counting on you!
(Lays down microphone. Walks to the side of the chancel, stops with back to Jim.)

SON: *(Comes to the chancel, picks up microphone.)*
Hey, Dad, guess what I just heard on the radio. The Los Angeles Lakers are in town tonight to play an exhibition game and there are still tickets left. Can you imagine Kareem Abdul-Jabbar and Magic Johnson in person? Can we go, Dad? Can we? It'll be just like old times when we used to do lots of things together. Fathers and sons should spend time together. So this is really important to me. Will you get the tickets? I'm counting on you, Dad!
(Lays down the microphone. Walks to the side of the chancel, stops with back to Jim.)

FRIEND: *(Comes to the chancel, picks up microphone.)*
Well, hello, old friend. Where have you been keeping yourself? We haven't got together in a long time. You used to call and we would eat lunch together. Seems you don't have time for your friends anymore. Hey, buddy, let me tell you—friends are important, but it's got to be a two-way street. But let's forget all that. Why don't we get together and play some tennis tonight? Two good friends just having fun. Boy, that sounds great. Tennis then, tonight. I'm counting on you!
(Lays down microphone. Walks to the side of the chancel, stops with back to Jim.)

PERSON REPRESENTING WORLD CONCERNS: *(Comes to chancel and picks up microphone.)*
The world is going to blow up right in your face. This arms race is suicidal. Nuclear weapons are insane. What is the church doing about it? What are you doing about it? You just sit here. Then you get up there on Sunday morning and preach your sweet little syrupy sermons because you are afraid of offending someone. Well, I'm telling you there is a disarmament meeting tonight and if you have one ounce of Christian conviction and courage left in you, you'll be there! I'm counting on you!
(Lays down microphone. Walks to the side of the chancel, stops with back to Jim.)

WIFE: *(Comes to the chancel and picks up microphone.)*
What do you mean you are not going to be home tonight? You promised me two weeks ago you would stay home tonight. This was to be our night—together—alone—just

68

you and me. Doesn't being with your wife mean anything to you anymore? Doesn't our relationship mean anything to you anymore? You act as if you love all those other people more than you love me. You promised you would be home tonight and I'm going to hold you to it. I'm counting on you! *(Lays down the microphone. Walks to the side of the chancel, stops with back to Jim. All the people pause, then all turn at once and come back toward Jim, saying their lines all at the same time very loudly. After about ten seconds the organ comes in with morbid and chaotic sounds.)*

JIM: God! Don't you care?
(All is silent, all freeze in position.)

GOD: Shalom.
(Participants fade away to their seats.)

JIM: What?

GOD: I said, "Shalom."

JIM: Who is that? Now, who wants a piece of me?

GOD: I am who I am.

JIM: Oh, hello, God.

GOD: Hello, James.

JIM: Where have you been?

GOD: I have told you, "I am with you always."

JIM: Well, what good does that do me?

GOD: It does not do you any good unless you are willing to be aware of my presence.

JIM: Oh, this is just great. First of all I have all these people pulling at me from all different sides, each of them wanting a piece of me. There are the responsibilities at the church, my mother, my son, my friends, the world's problems and my wife. I feel as if I am being torn apart, and now you. What do you want from me?

GOD: **I have brought you a gift.**

JIM: A gift?

GOD: **Yes, a gift.**

JIM: Well, what is it?

GOD: **Shalom.**

JIM: Shalom? Isn't that the Jewish word for good-by?

GOD: **The word is often used for a greeting or for when two people are separating.**

JIM: Are you leaving me? Are you running out on me? Is that it? You've stopped by to say "Shalom," good-by, pal, you're on your own?

GOD: **No, James, I am not leaving you and you are not on your own.**

JIM: Well, why have you brought me the word "Shalom"?

GOD: **I have not brought you the word, I have brought you the gift of Shalom.**

JIM: Well, let's see it then. Put it up here on the desk.

GOD: **It doesn't go on the desk. It goes inside of you. I have brought you the gift of Shalom. I have brought inner peace for your life.**

JIM: Well, it certainly is a timely gift. My insides are a shambles. My stomach is always tied up in knots. Some people talk about having butterflies in their stomach. Well, my butterflies think they are kamikaze pilots. Inner peace? My insides are just pure . . . pure . . . .

GOD: **Chaos?**

JIM: Yes, chaos. That's a good word to describe it.

GOD: Chaos has always been a part of life. Before there was life there was chaos. It was out of chaos that I began my creation. I created the sun and the moon. It was out of chaos that I created the earth with the waters and the land. It was out of chaos that I created the vegetation and the animals of the land and the birds of the air and the fish of the sea. It was out of chaos that I created man and woman to have dominion over everything else that I created. In order that man and woman might be able to exist with that responsibility, out of choas I created shalom—peace.

JIM: I don't understand.

GOD: On the seventh day I created the sabbath—a day of rest—a day of shalom. It was the culmination of my creation.

JIM: Do you mean that I have to struggle through life with all its pressures and responsibilities all week long and wait till Sunday to experience any peace?

GOD: No, the story of my performing the creation in seven days is a symbolic way of explaining the sense of order within my creation. The sabbath or day of sha-lom is the crowning act, that means all of my cre-ation—all of life—can experience the sense of shalom each day, each moment. Jesus said, "You were not created for the sabbath, the sabbath was created to serve you." You need the experience of the sabbath in each moment of your life. As a part of my creation not only can you experience it, it is a part of my own design for you to experience shalom.

JIM: But I am not experiencing it now. My whole life seems to be tossing about like a ship in a storm at sea.

GOD: Once when my son, Jesus, was in the physical form on earth, he had been teaching a large crowd all day and as the evening came he and his disciples got into a boat and set out to cross the Sea of Galilee. He was tired from the day's activities and he fell asleep. While he was sleeping, a great storm came up and great waves were beating against the boat and the boat began to fill with water. The disciples in the boat began to panic as people often do in the midst of chaos and they woke Jesus with the same question that you screamed to me a few minutes ago, "Don't you care?" Jesus awoke and spoke these words, "Shalom, peace! Be still!" and the storm was quieted and the fear left the disciples as they were filled with awe by his power. That power is available to you—shalom.

JIM: Are you trying to say that you will calm all the storms around me? That you will cause all those people to leave me alone? That you will take away all the pressures and demands in my life?

GOD: No, that is not what I am saying. The chaos, pressures and demands will always be a part of your existence. You see, you have missed the point of the story. The important storms that were quieted that evening were the storms of fear and anxiety and sense of being alone that were raging inside of the disciples. Those storms were quieted and replaced by shalom.

JIM: Well, what are you waiting for? You said you brought me the gift of shalom. Go ahead, quiet my storms. Put the gift of shalom inside me.

GOD: I can't do that.

JIM: What? You said you brought the gift of shalom to me. You said it goes inside of me. Why can't you put it there?

GOD: I cannot put it inside of you because it is already there. The gift of shalom is a part of my creation, it is a part of you. It is there because I love you and because you need it to deal with the chaos in your life. But as long as you go running madly about from one crisis to another, trying to meet every demand placed upon you, succumbing to every pressure that comes your way, never stopping long enough even to be aware of the power of my presence, then you will never experience the shalom that can be yours—that is yours.

JIM: Well, how can I experience it then?

GOD: **As you feel that pressure building and the storms starting to blow and the chaos getting to you, stop and remember this line, "Be still then and know that I am God." And remember the "I" in that statement refers to me, not you. I am God, you are not. To survive in the midst of chaos you need the experience of shalom, but to experience it you must stop long enough to be aware of my presence—to partake of the sabbath.**

JIM: Thank you, God. I feel better already. Well, I'd better get busy and decide how many of those things I can squeeze into tonight. We'll talk again sometime.

GOD: **James, I have told you I am with you always. Be still and know that *I* am God.** *(Pause)*

JIM: Shalom.

GOD: **Shalom.**

10

"The Path of Discipleship: Sharing the Good News"

John 4:27–42

(Table and chair are set in the middle of the chancel. The table serves as a desk. Papers and telephone on the table. Jim comes in and sits down, picks up the phone and dials.)

JIM: Hey, David, how are you doing? . . . Fine. I was just sitting here starting to work on some stuff and was thinking about the movie that Pat and I saw last night and I just had to tell you about it. *On Golden Pond.* Have you seen it? . . . Oh, you have got to go see this movie. It is great. An Academy Award winner you know. And with Henry Fonda, Katherine Hepburn and Jane Fonda you just can't go wrong. . . . Well, yes it has some language that will bother some people, but the story, the scenery and acting are so great that I would really urge you to go see it. Well, Henry Fonda is the crusty old professor and Katherine Hepburn is his wife and she really understands him and they banter back and forth, but they really have a strong relationship. Jane Fonda is his daughter and they have never had that good a relationship and well, I'm not going to tell you the whole story. Anyway Pat and I enjoyed it so much that we want to go see it again next Saturday and we wanted to invite you and

Alice to go with us. . . . Hey, that's great. We'll pick you up Saturday at seven. OK? . . . Well, I'll get back to work. Talk to you later. Bye.

GOD: Hello, James.
(Jim looks around and then continues to work.)

Hello, James.

JIM: Who is that?

GOD: I am who I am.

JIM: Oh, hello, God.

GOD: How are you doing?

JIM: Fine.

GOD: James, I'm not interested in your one-word, flip answers. How are you doing?

JIM: Really pretty well. I have been working on that idea of shalom since we talked last fall and it has really helped. I am more relaxed. I just wish you would come around more often so we could have more of these talks.

GOD: I have told you I am with you always.

JIM: Oh, that's right.

GOD: What are you doing?

JIM: Oh, I am hard at work here on church things.

GOD: It sounded as if you were hard at work.

JIM: Oh, the phone conversation; well, I just took a quick break to call David to tell him about a movie Pat and I saw last night. But I was going to get right back to work on church stuff. But the movie was so great I just had to tell him about it. It had Henry Fonda, Jane Fonda and Katherine Hepburn in it—some of my favorite actors!

75

GOD: Yes, they are good, but I prefer George Burns myself. Tell me, James. Why didn't you wait until Sunday after worship to tell David about the movie?

JIM: Because I was excited about it. I wanted to tell him now.

GOD: Is that the only reason?

JIM: No, he isn't a member of our church. He won't be here Sunday.

GOD: In what church is he involved?

JIM: Well, he doesn't go to church.

GOD: Why won't he be here Sunday?

JIM: I just said he doesn't go to any church.

GOD: Did he turn you down when you invited him?

JIM: Well, uh . . . I didn't invite him.

GOD: Why not?

JIM: I just said, he doesn't go to church.

GOD: That's not what I asked. Why didn't you invite him?

JIM: Well . . . because . . . wait a minute. I can't just go around inviting everyone to come to church. People would think I'm some kind of religious fanatic. You have to have a good relationship with people to invite them to church.

GOD: Do you have a good relationship with David?

JIM: Yes.

GOD: Then I ask again, why didn't you invite him?

JIM: Well, I guess I would be a little embarrassed to do that.

GOD: I embarrass you?

JIM: No. No, you don't embarrass me.

GOD: **Your church embarrasses you?**

JIM: No, the church doesn't embarrass me. We have a great church. I'm proud of our church.

GOD: **Why, then, would you be embarrassed?**

JIM: I'm not sure; it's just a feeling that I have down inside of me. Every time I think about inviting someone to come to church my stomach just knots up. Maybe I am afraid that people will associate me with those fundamentalists who are always trying to force their religion on others.

GOD: **Do you usually let other people's actions or methods dictate to you what you will do?**

JIM: No, but their approach just turns me off and I think it turns other people off, too.

GOD: **So what you're saying is that it isn't what they are doing but the way they are doing it that bothers you. It just isn't you.**

JIM: That's right.

GOD: **Then why don't you be you? You don't have to do things the way other people do them. Just be yourself. That's all I am asking. A little while ago you were willing to tell David all about a movie and invite him to go with you to see it. Why not invite him to come with you to church just like you did to the movie?**

JIM: Well, there is another problem.

GOD: **And what is that?**

JIM: What you are talking about is evangelism. Winning people to Christ and all that, sharing my faith, and to be quite honest, my faith is a little shaky sometimes.

GOD: **I know.**

JIM: Well, you know then that I really am not the person to be doing that. I would like to, but I just am not ready to do that. Last week at church we started our Lenten program of The Path of Discipleship. I think I would be more comfortable if I waited until I was a little farther along the path myself before I started to try to convince others that they should accept Jesus as their Lord and Savior.

GOD: **Where did you get that word "convince"? All we've been talking about is inviting.**

JIM: Well, isn't that what evangelism is all about, convincing other people to become Christians?

GOD: **No. You have the areas of responsibility mixed up. Whether or not persons become Christians involved in a local community of faith is up to them. It is _their_ responsibility, not yours. You don't have to convince anyone. _Your_ responsibility is to _invite_ them. Putting it in terms of your Lenten program, it is _your_ responsibility to invite them to share the path of discipleship with you. It is _their_ responsibility to _decide_ if they will do it. You can't be responsible for someone else's decisions and actions, only for your own. Do you remember the scripture that was used for last week's sermon?**

JIM: Yes, it was about the Samaritan woman who met Jesus at the well and he offered her the living water.

GOD: **Do you remember what happened after that?**

JIM: Well, I think she . . . uh . . . she . . . uh . . .

GOD: **Get your Bible out, James. Turn to John 4:27.**

JIM: John 4:27.

GOD: **That's in the New Testament.**

JIM: I knew that. Here it is.

GOD: **Read.**

78

JIM: "At that moment Jesus' disciples returned, and they were greatly surprised to find him talking with a woman. But none of them said to her, 'What do you want?' or asked him, 'Why are you talking with her?'

"Then the woman left her water jar, went back to the town, and said to the people there, 'Come and see the man who told me everything I have ever done. Could he be the Messiah?' So they left the town and went to Jesus." *(TEV)*

GOD: **Now, put the Bible down and tell me what she did.**

JIM: Well, after talking to Jesus she went back to town and . . . and *invited* the people to come and see Jesus.

GOD: **That's right. She didn't *try* to convince them. She simply invited them. Now I admit she was probably enthusiastic in her invitation—just as you were with your invitation to the movie, but the point is that she invited. In her invitation she raised the question. "Could he be the Messiah?" That was a question they would have to answer for themselves. So they accepted her invitation and came. Now skip down to verse 40 and read on.**

JIM: "So when the Samaritans came to him, they begged him to stay with them and Jesus stayed there two days. Many more believed because of his message, and they told the woman, 'We believe now, not because of what you said, but because we ourselves have heard him, and we know that he really is the Saviour of the world.'" *(TEV)*

GOD: **You see they accepted Jesus, not because of what *she* said but because of what they experienced once they got there. They would never have had that experience if she hadn't been willing to invite them.**

JIM: I guess I had never seen that scripture as an evangelism scripture before. She invited. They decided.

GOD: **I want your friend David to be a part of a community of faith. I want him to come and worship. *He* is a child of mine and I want him to be in relationship to me. I want him to be on the path of discipleship. The decision is *his*. I don't force *anyone,* but first someone has to invite him.**

JIM: *(Pause — looks at the telephone.)*
Ah, if you would excuse me. I think I have a phone call to make. As always it has been a learning experience to talk to you. We will talk again soon.

GOD: James, I have told you I am with you always.

JIM: Right. *(Picks up receiver — dials.)* David, I have someplace else that I want to invite you to go with me . . . .

11

"God, I'm Growing Old"

Luke 1:5–20

(Chancel is set with breakfast table. Jim comes out limping. He pours a cup of coffee and then sits down slowly as if his muscles are really sore.)

JIM: Oh . . . my leg is so sore. It feels as if I pulled a muscle in the softball game last night. My whole body aches. God, I'm growing old. God, I'm growing old.

GOD: Hello, James.

JIM: *(Looks around.)*

GOD: Hello, James.

JIM: Who is that?

GOD: I am who I am.

JIM: Oh, hello, God.

GOD: You seem surprised to hear from me.

JIM: Well, there is usually a little more time in between these talks of ours. You usually don't come around this often.

GOD: James, I have told you I am with you always.

JIM: Right.

GOD: How are things going?

JIM: Oh, fine.

GOD: What was all that moaning then that I heard?

JIM: Oh that. Well, I played softball with the church team last night and . . . well . . . the old body just doesn't bounce back the way it used to.

GOD: So?

JIM: Well, they say, "you are only as old as you feel" and this morning I feel old.

GOD: So your body is telling you that you are growing older.

JIM: It sure is. You know, a couple of years ago I had to give up basketball. I mean, my mind still had visions of my flying through the air toward the basket, but my body just went tripping along the floor. Now . . . now I am beginning to wonder about softball. My hitting is still OK and I suppose I could pitch until I was sixty, but the problem is running around the bases. They seem farther apart than they used to. You don't suppose you could kind of help me along from second to third base do you?

GOD: James.

JIM: You know, just kind of lift me up . . . .

GOD: James!

JIM: Make my legs go a little faster . . . .

GOD: James!!!

JIM: Uh, I suppose you don't work that way, do you?

GOD: No James, I do not work that way! But I am willing to listen to you tell me more about your feelings about growing older.

JIM: Well, I will be thirty-nine this summer and I realize that to many people that is still young, but I can remember as I was growing up that Jack Benny always talked about being 39 and I thought that was old. That also means that next year I will hit the big 4-0—forty years old!! Why, the age our kids are, it is possible that within ten years I could be a grandfather. Me a grandfather.

GOD: Being a grandfather bothers you?

JIM: Well, there is an old joke that goes, "I don't mind being a grandfather. I'm just not sure I want to live with a grandmother." That's another thing that is changing.

GOD: What is that?

JIM: My enjoyment of age jokes. I used to be great at kidding my older friends about their ages, but those jokes aren't as funny as they used to be. I remember giving Pat a surprise one-third of a century birthday party. That was really funny at thirty-three and a third, but at thirty-nine it isn't quite so funny. On my friend Joe's fortieth birthday the staff gave him a party and for presents we gave him Geritol, Polygrip and Grecian Formula. We had a wheelchair for him to sit in, and Pat made him a cake that had a hill in the middle of it with this figure of a man starting down the other side of the hill. Oh it was hilarious . . . then!

GOD: You sound really bothered by growing older.

JIM: Well, I've read where the experts claim middle age begins at thirty-five, but I have just kind of laughed that off, but there is no way to deny that forty is middle age and when you reach middle age you get into that midlife crisis thing.

GOD: Midlife crisis?

JIM: Yes, that's where men in their early forties start thinking about what they have accomplished or haven't accomplished in their life, and go a little crazy trying to reestablish or hang on to their youth.

GOD: And you think you are going to go a little crazy?

JIM: Well, I suppose it's possible, but, no, I think I'll probably handle it OK.

GOD: Well then, what is *really* bothering you?

JIM: I guess, for the first time, I'm looking down the road and seeing that I really am, one day, going to be old. I mean old.

GOD: And that frightens you?

JIM: You bet it does.

GOD: Why? What does it mean to you to be old?

JIM: Well, for one thing it means retirement.

GOD: What about retirement?

JIM: I can't imagine myself retiring. How can I just sit around and do nothing? I've been active all my life. I'm afraid that Pat and I would get on each other's nerves if we were together twenty-four hours a day. I'm afraid of boredom. I'm afraid of what it would do to my identity because our identity is so tied up in what we do for a living. I'm afraid that I would die. I have heard the stories of men dying within months after retiring. I'm afraid . . . I'm just afraid of retiring.

GOD: Retiring from a job or profession is no problem. The problem comes when they retire from life. If my people could see that retirement is simply one more transition in life and not the end of life they could approach it with a much better attitude. In addition, it is a transition for which you can make some plans. Retirement is not a reward for a life of hard work, nor is it a punishment. It must be viewed simply as a different part of your life to do with as you choose, just like any other part of life. You chose to be married, you chose to be a parent, you chose to be a minister, and in retirement you can choose to be bored or involved. What else does old mean to you?

JIM: Well, it means a nursing home. I don't want to give up my independent living and be stuck away in a nursing home.

GOD: **What do you mean stuck away? How can you say stuck away when the people there with whom you will be living are my children? You see, James, I'm not so interested in where you are living as I am about *how* you are living. There will be people there to talk to. There will be people there to listen to. There will be people there to help and *I* will be there.**

Now I know that nobody likes to give up independent living, but if the time comes for you that you must, your basic Christian love of me and of your neighbor will continue. It may just be that your neighbors are a little closer than they have been. What else does old mean to you?

JIM: Useless. I read and hear so many old people say that they feel useless—that they have been put on a shelf. They can't do what they used to do. They just feel useless.

GOD: **Uselessness is a state of mind. There is a story in the New Testament about two of my children who were very old. Their names were Zechariah and Elizabeth. They believed that they were way too old to have a child, but I needed them. I needed them to have a child who would foretell the coming of my Son. They had that child and they nurtured him and raised him in the faith and he became John the Baptist.**

I need people of all ages to do many different things in this world for me. No one ever gets too old to be of service. They may not physically be able to do some of the things they used to do, but they can still do the things I have for them to do. No one gets too old to live a Christian life in a world that needs it desperately.

JIM: I am beginning to feel a little better.

GOD: **Life is full of changes. As you get older, your perception of life changes, your knowledge changes, your priorities change, your attitudes change. Most of the time that is called maturing. There is great value in the maturing process and my older children have a great deal to offer this world. I am counting on them to**

continue to be my servants in this world. The world needs them and I need them.

JIM: Well, I thank you again for these talks. They always help. If you happen to be around on my fortieth birthday maybe you could remind me of what you said today.

GOD: James, I have told you I am with you always.

JIM: Right, I'll remember.

12

"Don't Send God"

2 Corinthians 2:14–16

(Table and chair serve as an office setting. Telephone on desk. Jim comes in and sits down, shuffles some papers, sighs and spends a couple of moments in silence. Then picks up the phone.)

JIM: Ruth, I need a few minutes of quiet time. Would you hold my calls for a while, please? Thanks.
(Pause—bowing head) O God, O God, there are so many needs in this world, so many things that need your attention. There are people at war, there are people who are hungry, there are people out of work, there are people who are emotionally hurting, there are people who are spiritually floundering with no church home—no value base in their lives. O God, where are you? Your people need you. Don't you care anymore? O God, O God.

GOD: Hello, James.

JIM: *(Picking up the phone)* Ruth, I asked for you to hold my calls. *(Then looking quizzically at the phone)* Hello, Hello. *(Puts the phone back down.)*

GOD: Hello, James.

JIM: Who is that?

87

GOD: I am who I am.

JIM: Oh, hello, God. Oh, God. I was just talking to you.

GOD: I know.

JIM: Well, I didn't expect to hear from you.

GOD: I have been trying to talk to you.

JIM: You have? I didn't hear you.

GOD: That's the trouble with your prayers, James; you do so much talking you never have time to listen.

JIM: Well, there is a lot to tell you about.

GOD: Do you think that I do not know what is going on in *my* world?

JIM: Oh, no . . . I mean yes—sure you do, but there are so many things that I am concerned about and I thought if I could just bring them to your attention then maybe you might go and do something about them.

GOD: Do something about them?

JIM: Yes, you know, take care of them, solve the problems, cure the ills, whip this world into shape . . . uh . . . work a few miracles.

GOD: Work a few miracles? Do you mean like abracadabra? Is that what you think I am, James, a magician?

JIM: Well, no . . . but . . . you have done a few miracles in the past—the creating of this wonderful world, that was a miracle—the separating of the Red Sea when the Hebrew people were escaping bondage in Egypt, that was a miracle—and others. See, you have done miracles and a few well placed miracles today would help this world a great deal.

GOD: Funny you should mention that. I have been working on a few new miracles but I am having some trouble with them.

88

JIM: You're having trouble? You who created the world and everything in it? You're having trouble?

GOD: **Oh, that. That was easy compared to the miracle I'm working on now. This is a tough one.**

JIM: But you're all powerful. You can do anything.

GOD: **No, James, I am not all powerful; that is, I have chosen to restrict my power. I have created you and all my people with a free will. I cannot force you to do anything. I can only tell you what I want done. The decision of whether or not to do it is up to you.**

JIM: Well, what is this miracle you are working on that is so tough?

GOD: **To get my people to quit trying to send me to do what _they_ can be doing themselves. That is the miracle I am working on.**

JIM: I don't understand.

GOD: **My people have become lazy. You have become lazy, James. How easy it is for you to sit here in your nice office, close your eyes and bow your head and allow me into your life for a few minutes through _what you call_ prayer. You read off a list of all the things in the world that you think need attention and then send me off like a messenger boy to take care of them, or, as you say, solve the problems, cure the ills, whip the world into shape and work a few miracles. Well, that will _not_ get the job done, James. I don't work that way. And it is _not_ the way that I want you to work.**

JIM: Do you mean that I shouldn't bring my concerns to you in prayer?

GOD: **No, that is not what I mean. You may bring anything to me. You may share anything with me. You can share your hopes, your failures, your successes, your doubts, your concerns—anything—and I will listen, but you act as though that's all you have to do. Just identify the problem and then you expect me to take** care of it. You act as if you are supposed to point out the hungry and then I am to feed them; you are supposed to point out the thirsty and I am to give them drink. You act as if you are supposed to point out the strangers and I am supposed to welcome them; you point out the naked and I am to clothe them. You point out the sick and those in prison, and I am supposed to visit them. Quite convenient for you, James. But that is not what Jesus had in mind in that parable.

JIM: I know. That's always been one of my favorite pieces of scripture. I have used it often for sermons, but I don't think I have ever felt the point of it quite as much as I just did.

GOD: Talk to me about that scripture.

JIM: Well, Jesus is saying that there are a lot of people in need—the hungry, the thirsty, the naked, and so on, and that out of our Christian commitment we are to meet those needs. Basically, Jesus is saying that however we treat those people in need is how we treat him. If we help them we are helping him; if we ignore them we are ignoring him.

GOD: Good. You have an excellent intellectual understanding of the scripture—now all you have to do is put it into practice instead of sending me to do your work.

JIM: Right.

GOD: I want you to take a look at another piece of scripture. It is not so well known as the other. In fact you have never preached a sermon on it, but Paul really had a good insight into how I work when he wrote this letter. Take your Bible there and look up Second Corinthians *(pause)*. That's right after First Corinthians. *(Pause)*. Second chapter, verses 14 through 16. Now read that out loud.

JIM: "But thanks be to God, who in Christ always leads us in triumph, and through us spreads the fragrance of the knowledge of him everywhere. For we are the aroma of Christ to God among those who are being saved and among those who are perishing, to one a fragrance from death to

90

death, to the other a fragrance from life to life. Who is sufficient for these things?"

GOD: **Now, talk to me about that scripture.**

JIM: Well, first of all I see that you are always with us because it says you lead us in triumph.

GOD: **That's right. I do not want you to send me off to do your work, but that does not mean you have to go off to do it by yourself either. I will be with you as always. Go on.**

JIM: Well, it says that the fragrance of the knowledge of God will be spread.

GOD: **Wait a minute, back up. How is that fragrance spread? Do I spread it?**

JIM: Well, in a way. Paul says you spread it through us.

GOD: **That's right, I need you as my instrument. It is through you that I accomplish my goal. But you have the freedom of choice. If you choose not to do it, or simply sit there at your desk trying to send me, then my goal will never be accomplished. Go on.**

JIM: We are the aroma of God. Some will perceive that aroma as a life-giving scent, but others will fight it as they would the scent of death.

GOD: **See, I told you Paul knew what he was talking about here. As you try to help those people in need or try to speak to those moral issues that are confronting my world, some will welcome you with open arms, others will welcome you with the same enthusiasm they have for death. Now, read verse 17.**

JIM: "For we are not, like so many, peddlers of God's word; but as men of sincerity, as commissioned by God, in the sight of God we speak in Christ."

GOD: You see, James, it is out of your sincerity of faith that you must reach out. *You* are commissioned by me to do *my* work. Just as Jesus said, "Go ye into all the world." He didn't say, "God will go into all the world." He said, "Go *ye* into all the world. I will be there with you." As Paul said, ". . . . in the sight of God we speak in Christ."

JIM: Whew — I think it is easier to send you.

GOD: *(sympathetically)* **Yes, it is easier.**

JIM: I also think you are right. I have been lazy.

GOD: **I'm *glad* you think I'm *right,* James.**

JIM: I see why this miracle is such a tough one to pull off. You can't do it on your own. I have to decide, too.

GOD: **Correct!**

JIM: It's not that I don't care. I really am concerned about the hungry and the tendency for war and violence in our world. I ache when I think of those who are hurting and those who are spiritually floundering with no church home and no value base in their lives. I really do.

GOD: *(sympathetically)* **I know you do.**

JIM: What am I going to do?

GOD: ***That* is the question, James. What *are* you going to do? It is the answer to that question that I am waiting to hear from you and from *all* of my children that call themselves—Christian.** *(Pause)*

JIM: Well, I guess I have some deciding to do. Again it was nice talking to you. See you again sometime.

GOD: **James, I have said I am with you always.**

JIM: Right, I'll remember.

GOD: **I am also waiting!**